Dear Mike,

Great to see you in India. Enjoy reading this book which is the essence of operational Excellence in BPO!

P. G. Raghuraman
June 26, 2009.

The Obvious Office

A step by step plan to
dramatically improve your
business performance

Andy Hobson

CORVUS SERVICES

Copyright © 2006 Andy Hobson
The right of Andy Hobson to be identified
as Author of this book has been asserted
by him in accordance with the Copyright,
Designs and Patents Act 1988.

First published 2006 in the UK by
Corvus Services
Seago House
13 Christchurch Road
Norwich NR2 2AE
Tel: +44(0)1603 507647
www.obviousoffice.com

Reprinted in 2008, 2009

ISBN 0-9552746-0-5
A CIP catalogue record of this book can be
obtained from the British Library.

Book design Hotbrand
Illustrations Alan Batley
Printed and bound by
Crowes Complete Print

Contents

Acknowlegements

Putting this book together has been a team effort and I am deeply grateful to the following people who put up with my naivety and made this book possible.

Caroline Merz took my initial draft and knocked it into shape. She advised on the overall structure of the book and massaged my words into a more readable and clearer form. When I struggled to find the right words to express an idea, she always provided an elegant solution. Caroline can be contacted at caroline.merz@ntlworld.com

Alan Batley is an extraordinary modelmaker and illustrator. His work brought the book to life, helping to give it a warmth and accessibility. He listened patiently as I attempted to explain the message I wanted to put across and then came up with the great images that illustrate the book's concepts so well. Alan can be contacted at abatley60@yahoo.com

Kevin Jones at Hotbrand has managed this project from the very beginning. When I was contemplating putting something together under the Obvious Office umbrella, he designed the interlocking rings logo. He then provided the creative input for the book design, working closely with Alan on the illustrations and coming up with the stunning cover design. Finally, he project managed all the mechanical and legal steps needed to turn the words and illustrations into a printed book. Kevin can be contacted at kevin@hot-brand.com

Why I wrote this book

I must be a glutton for punishment. Why? Because for over 25 years I managed factories. I spent every waking hour trying to satisfy extremely demanding customers who could buy from anywhere in the world. And boy was it tough. They demanded - and got - superlative levels of quality, and immediate and flexible responses to their needs. Oh, and let's not forget the year-on-year price reductions we had to make, or risk losing the work.

How can you do this and still stay in business? With great difficulty. Many factories have closed in the face of such demands. But many others survive and thrive despite the odds, and people like me from the manufacturing sector know how to do it.

In the last three years, I have worked in offices helping them improve what they do. I have applied manufacturing performance improvement techniques to the office workplace, and the results are staggering:

- *the time taken to do the work has been reduced from weeks to days and hours*

- *error rates have been reduced to almost zero*

- *costs have been slashed - by up to two thirds in some offices*

I have proved that the tried and tested techniques used by world class manufacturing companies to survive and prosper in a highly competitive world can easily be used in offices to deliver step changes in performance.

Because the techniques used are so simple, they can be used by anyone who works in an office. Indeed, benefits are usually greatest when the people who actually do the work are intimately involved in making that work better.

Why should offices learn from factories?

Let's look at some facts:

FACT: The UK Consumer Price Index has risen by over 80% since 1987. We're used to paying a bit more for everything each year.

FACT: Services cost significantly more than they used to.

- *a night out that cost £10 in 1987 is likely to cost over £32 in 2005*
- *to get something fixed that cost £30 in 1987 could cost you nearly £90 today*
- *the same goes for insurance, car repairs, local and national government services, and many more items*

FACT: Despite this, many of the goods we buy are hardly any more expensive than they were in 1987 – and some are even less expensive.

- *a fridge costing £100 or a cooker costing £300 in 1987 can both be bought for less than that in 2005*
- *a car equivalent to the one you spent £8000 on in 1987 can be bought today for less than £10,000 - and it's a much better vehicle*

How can this be?

We all know about TVs, DVD players and PCs selling for rock-bottom prices. This can be explained by the twin effects of increasing demand and new technology. And, of course. a lot of things are now made in low-wage economies rather than in the West.

But...

A large number of common goods such as freezers and central heating systems that we all buy are still made in the high-wage economies of the West. The basic technology used in many common items has barely changed in 50 years, and demand for these items has grown only slowly.

So why should consumer durables such as fridges and cookers be actually lower in price now than they were in 1987 - and at the same time be far more reliable, have more features, and get delivered more quickly? And how can cars be only just over 10% more expensive than 10 years ago, even though they now come loaded with extras undreamt of in the 1980s, are better built and equipped, and need servicing at less frequent mileage intervals?

In real terms, because of the effects of inflation, cars and consumer durables are actually much cheaper to buy today than 20 years ago.

Is technology the answer?

Of course manufacturers have used technology to improve their operations, but isn't the same technology available to everybody? Aren't computers and high speed communications now used pretty much universally?

Unlike manufacturing or distribution organisations, those in the service sector don't have to physically move goods around or process and assemble material. So surely they should have reaped even more benefit from using new technology?

Survival of the fittest

The plain fact is that intense global competition helps drive down prices in manufacturing. Some organisations wither and die when faced with such competition. The survivors have learnt how to achieve the seemingly impossible: improve service and delivery, while at the same time reducing costs.

Where competition is weak or non-existent, the desperate need to reduce costs and improve service in order simply to survive does not exist. Compared to global manufacturing, retailing or distribution, great swathes of service organisations have little or no real competition. And where there is no competition, costs inexorably rise regardless of how well the organisation serves its clients or customers.

So what?

Now that we are becoming accustomed to a low-inflation environment and consumers have higher expectations, banks, insurance companies and other service companies who are finding it increasingly difficult to grow profits are looking towards the manufacturing sector to see if some of the lessons learned there can be used in an office setting.

And guess what - it works. They are starting to enjoy significant benefits by applying lessons learned in factories, not just in terms of customer service but also in drastically reducing the costs associated with providing that service.

Lessons for everyone

Why stop at financial services when these tools and techniques can be applied in every office environment? These same lessons can be, and have been, applied to healthcare organisations, local government, law firms, government agencies, police authorities - and, indeed, everywhere that groups of people in offices are doing something that has some value.

But I have also learnt that blindly applying tools that work in factories in an office setting often delivers hardly any benefits at all. Why? Because there are many activities that are taken for granted in factories that barely exist in offices. People working in factories know what they are making, know how to make it and have a pretty good idea how many to make and what resources are needed to make them.

When I talk to people working in offices I find that:

- *they often have no idea why they do what they do - there is no clear purpose*

- *they do the same work differently from others in the same office*

- *they have no idea of how much work to expect and don't know how many people are going to be needed to do the work*

- *the office is organised with no regard to the way work happens*

- *no-one really knows what is going on, and important information about work is non-existent*

- *problems are rarely fixed - they're either ignored or cumbersome work-rounds are put in place*

The Obvious Office

This book describes the six stages that I use to transform office performance. Each step addresses a key problem found in every office. Using jargon-free language and clear visual examples, the book will explain how to create an office where it is

- **obvious** *what the office does*
- **obvious** *how the office works*
- **obvious** *who does what*
- **obvious** *how you can get the work done, correctly and on time*
- **obvious** *how much better the office is performing; and lastly,*
- **obvious** *what the office can do to get even better*

Keep It Simple Stupid

The KISS principle is liberally used throughout the book. There really is nothing new in this book whatsoever... you might even say that the contents themselves are screamingly obvious.

For some readers the ideas will be new, but once they are explained you will probably think you knew all about it anyway.

For other readers, the contents will remind you of stuff that you should never really have stopped doing.

But the power of using all these simple, cheap, obvious techniques all together, all the time, is staggering.

The Obvious Office is a great place to work, where ordinary people using ordinary techniques produce extraordinary

Why I wrote this book

Chapter One

The Typical Office

What do you see when you walk into a typical office?

Normally, you expect to see:

- *people*
- *desks*
- *cupboards*
- *cabinets*
- *notice boards*
- *a drinks machine*
- *printers*
- *at least one photocopier*
- *a computer on every desk*

And, of course, paper and more paper everywhere you look.

And what are they all doing?

Most of the people will be sitting at their desks, staring into screens. Some may be on the telephone or reading something (possibly work-related). You might see a small group of people huddled round a VDU trying to sort something out. Somebody may be delivering really important documents. You might spot the odd person tearing their hair out because the photocopier is not working. There will almost certainly be somebody at the drinks machine getting a round of tea and coffee for their friends. And what would an office be without another bunch sitting around a table having a meeting?

Let's take a closer look...

1 Desks

These may be in small clusters or possibly, but increasingly rarely, set out in lines. On top of those desks will be a keyboard and mouse, a telephone, a desk tidy full of pens, highlighters, paperclips and other stuff amassed over the years.

Also on the desk there will be a mug or - more likely these days - a water bottle, stapler, Sellotape, Post-it notes, a photograph, tissues, cough sweets... I'm sure you can think of dozens of other possibilities for yourself.

Inside the desk pedestal cabinet lurk even more esoteric objects. Yes, there will be more pens, paperclips and everything else you saw on top of the desk, but in addition you will find copies of manuals, the bit of crumpled paper with the scrawled notes made when the desk owner started the job, a two-year-old newsletter, relics from the last office party, the hilarious photo of the office manager cross-

dressing for charity, magazines, a lunch pack (or more worryingly a lunch pack from last month festering in a long forgotten corner).

In fact you could find almost anything in a desk pedestal cabinet.

2 The rest of the office

If you walk around the office, you will find:

- *recycling bins;*

- *stocks of paper for the printer and photocopier;*

- *notices explaining what to do in the event of fire or how to protect your health at work or inviting you to join the office charity walk;*

- *a stirring message from the top boss who works somewhere very far away and who is only seen when the annual results video is shown to an awestruck audience.*

And - despite the ubiquitous use of computers - even more paper, filed away in cabinets and cupboards. You can't get away from it: all over the office, paper, paper and more paper. Whatever happened to the paperless office?

I could go on, but I'm sure you get the picture.

The universal office

I visit many offices and it always amazes me that no matter what the people in the office actually do, all offices somehow manage to look the same. They have the same things on the wall; they store things in pretty much the same way. Desks and what's on them are the same the world over.

Walk into any office anywhere and what does it tell you? Not a lot. You won't have the slightest clue as to what the office does. You will get no idea whether the organisation is busy, or whether it's going through a quiet patch. You're given little or no indication of whether everybody is in, whether they are working on the most important stuff, achieving targets, how much work is complete and how much is waiting to be done... and so on.

Reality check

The plain truth is that of course offices exist for many reasons, and people working in offices do very different things. On their own or as a group, they may be approving an insurance claim, preparing legal documents, paying expenses, dealing with customer concerns, telephone selling, compiling internal reports, inspecting suspicious financial transactions, deciding social security entitlements, maintaining web sites, organising a PR campaign, designing a new car, planning a housing development... The list is endless - yet the offices these people work in will all look virtually identical.

Why do all offices look the same?

It's simple - no-one ever thinks that offices need to be different. No-one ever thinks that an office should be organised around the work. It never enters an office planner's mind that by considering the processes performed in the office, a different layout may make the office more productive.

Office managers have no experience of the benefits of having a workplace organised around the activities needing to be done. And supervisors never dream that their team could produce more if only they had everything they needed readily at hand, and could quickly check how to do the job, how much was still to get done and how well they were doing.

The obvious factory

It's all very different in a modern factory. Walk round any well-run factory and it is obvious what that factory does.

It is also obvious

- *what today's work is*
- *where tools are kept*
- *where material is stored*
- *how to go about each task*
- *where things go next*

When it comes to performance, it is obvious

- *whether targets for quality, delivery and cost are being achieved*
- *what work is outstanding*
- *whether customers are happy or not*
- *what problems there are*

And as for the staff, it is obvious

- *who is in work today*
- *who is trained and who is not*
- *what the safety record is*
- *when the next meeting is and what's on the agenda*
- *who has booked a holiday and when*

Good factories are organised around the manufacturing process, and everything that happens in that factory is focused on running the process as smoothly as possible.

Why are good factories like this?

Because they have learned many bitter and painful lessons as they have coped with the incessant demands for improved performance driven in the main by intense world-wide competition - as well as having to pay good wages and producing profits to keep investors happy. They have learned what works.

Good factories make things obvious because it helps them provide year-on-year improvements in performance, delivering many of the benefits we all enjoy as the things made in factories get cheaper, do a better job and are available effectively off the shelf.

OK, but what's that got to do with me?

... you might say. In a factory you can watch as products are made and see what is going on; you can see if a machine is stopped or if something has been rejected for poor quality. You can tell immediately if someone is missing because production simply stops. If someone is not properly trained, output slows. If the factory is running well things are made more quickly than if it is running poorly. But offices don't make anything; much of what they do is hidden inside a computer or noted on a bit of paper.

That's true, but...

wouldn't it be great if you could walk round your office and see how things are going? Suppose that instead of poring over computer reports and management accounts you could see at a glance if you were achieving delivery targets, maintaining service quality and keeping costs within budget.

Wouldn't you love to know that performance will be maintained or even improved? Just think how much easier managing an office could be if problems were immediately apparent by just looking around the office.

Wouldn't it be great to have an 'Obvious Office'?

Don't just dream about it

Yes it is great to have an Obvious Office, as an increasing number of people are finding out.

Many offices in a wide variety of sectors have adopted the principles described in this book with great success. And it really is not that difficult. Much of what you will read is very simple. But what it does need from you is an open mind, a desire to make things better, a willingness to change, no fear of failure, and a determination to challenge and change forever the status quo.

In this book you will learn about some of the nuts and bolts of creating an Obvious Office, but a book on its own doesn't make a difference. Only you and your colleagues can actually make the difference, so at the end of each chapter you will find space to record your impressions, queries, and, most importantly, actions.

Notes:

Notes:

Chapter Two

The Focused Office

What is a 'focused office'? It's an office where everybody is focused on what they're there to do. In a focused office, it's absolutely clear to both staff and visitors exactly what the purpose of that office is.

Once everybody knows what they are really at work to do, it becomes much easier to decide what needs to happen to do that job well and what else needs to happen to do that job better. You can then look at everything that happens in the office and ask yourselves one simple question:

"Is this what I am really here to do?"

If the answer is "yes", and what you are doing is actually directly useful for your customer, then do more of it.

If the answer is "no", and you are not actually doing anything useful for your customer, then you should either stop doing it or devote less time to it.

If you stop doing useless things you can spend more time doing useful things. If you spend more time doing useful things, you will please your customer and the office will improve. This is a good thing.

What are we here for?

The very first thing to do when creating an Obvious Office is to agree what the office is there for. That sounds easy, doesn't it? In reality, if you ask anybody working in a typical office what they do, they will tell you what task they perform: "I enter this data"; "I assess these applications", and so on. If you ask a supervisor the same question they will tell you about writing reports, attending meetings, organising training or handling problems.

In the typical office no-one ever tells you what the office is actually for; what useful task it accomplishes or what it does to help somebody else.

Until you can state in concrete, unambiguous terms exactly what the office is there to do, how is it possible to do it well? How can you expect people to deliver superlative service if they don't actually know what that service is?

No recycling

When you define what the office does, **please do not recycle the corporate mission statement.** What you want is something in plain language that describes what it is you all come to work to get done. This should be as simple, but as specific, as possible - and will always relate to a customer.

Now I know many people are uncomfortable with the word 'customer', but I use it because most people understand what it means. If you don't like 'customer', please use another word you feel happy with. But that word must describe the person or organisation that wants you to do whatever it is you do.

Who is the customer?

Sometimes the customer is easy to define. It's the person whose hard cash is paying your office to do something.

However, in many cases it is difficult to pinpoint exactly who the customer really is.

Find the customer - an example

Let's say you are working in telesales. Your job is to create a new customer or make a new sale to an existing customer.

You are probably selling some sort of benefit to a customer. The customer is only interested in getting that benefit. They are definitely not interested in what you actually do, namely:

1 *creating the order*

2 *performing a credit check*

3 *setting up a new account*

4 *updating the database*

You are not actually doing anything at the time of the sale that the customer really wants. They may have placed an order, but until the order is fulfilled that customer has received nothing.

So although telesales deals directly with a customer of the organisation, when you define what telesales does and who they do it for, telesales' real customer is not the person at the other end of the phone.

Telesales' real customer is likely to be someone within your own organisation who is responsible for making sales.

We now have a conundrum: when is a customer not a customer? When you don't actually do anything for them.

Confused?

Let's try and make things a bit clearer.

Imagine that the telesales function is contracted out to a specialist organisation. This organisation supplies the staff, equipment and software that other organisations buy, in order to promote sales.

Now it is very clear who the telesales' real customer is, and that customer wants you to get as many sales for the lowest possible cost without causing unnecessary difficulties with the people you are calling. The customer wants you to be polite, courteous and not upset anybody.

Another example

Imagine that you work in an office that is chasing unpaid bills.

You are dealing with 'customers' of the wider organisation. But your office's real customer is probably the owner of the organisation who wants you to recover as much debt as possible, at the lowest possible cost, even if in the long run that means the organisation's 'customer' becomes an 'ex-customer'.

How bad can it get?

I was working with some staff in the Human Resources department of a large government agency and asked them, "Who are your customers?"

They told me their customers were the staff working for the organisation who needed information or action from the team, and managers who wanted advice on recruitment. So far so good. But then, totally unprompted, the staff started to tell me about everybody else they worked for:

1 *the local Job Centre and recruitment agencies;*

2 *job applicants and other members of the public seeking information;*

3 *staff working for companies providing outsourced services to the organisation;*

4 *the Health and Safety Executive, Inland Revenue and other government agencies;*

5 *any third party requesting information about staff;*

6 *subcontractors and suppliers;*

... and the list went on.

When I then asked, "How do you know if you are doing a good job?" I got complete silence. Is it any wonder that this group were so disillusioned? How could they possibly provide the service they thought they should be providing to all these 'customers'?

Depending on exactly which task they performed, they really only had two customers - the staff and the managers. Everything else they did was actually something they did for one of these customers.

Remember

It is always worth taking the time and care to define who your office's 'real' customer is: never take this for granted. It may be the organisation's actual customer, that is, the person who is buying the product or service, or it may be someone within the organisation. Whoever it is, your office's customer will normally care very much that you do things well.

Which brings us to:

Important point number 1

The purpose of the Focused Office is to do something for your customer

No apologies for the simplicity of this. You might even think it is banal. But how many people in your office work with this purpose always in mind?

What is the office for?

Some examples of what people do in an office:

- *make sure bills are paid*
- *recruit staff*
- *handle insurance claims*
- *check for fraud*
- *organise social housing*
- *collect taxes*
- *resolve customer complaints*

'Useless' work

It is at this point that you will realise that there are many people, usually managers and supervisors, who do nothing of direct use to your customer. However, please do not prepare a Board Paper suggesting that all managerial grades should be removed immediately as they are useless (even if it's true).

Unfortunately, in any organisation there are things that simply have to be done in order for the organisation to exist. For example, compliance with legal and regulatory requirements is necessary for the organisation to operate. Offices need maintenance, in order to provide a suitable working environment. Somebody needs to make sure that basic disciplines are maintained. Checks are needed to reduce fraud. People need counselling and development - and there are many other vital jobs that need to be done that are not directly useful to your customer.

However, if you apply the rule that you should spend only the amount of time that is absolutely necessary to perform these 'useless' activities, you will then perhaps begin to reduce the amount of time spent on them.

Spend more time doing useful things and less time doing 'useless' things.

(You will learn more about reducing the amount of time spent doing 'useless' activities in chapter 7, The Improving Office.)

Keeping the customer happy

So, now you have defined what you're at work for. You know that if you spend more time doing what your customers want, and less time doing stuff that is useless to your customers, you will please your customers.

But how can you make absolutely sure that what you do will please them?

No matter what type of organisation you work for, there are only three things that matter to a customer:

1 *Is it what I wanted - is the* **QUALITY** *right?*

2 *Did it happen when I expected - was the* **DELIVERY** *right?*

3 *Did I get value for money - was the* **COST** *right?*

Quality, delivery and cost are the three things that matter to any customer. Depending on what you are doing, one of these may be more important than the others - but all three will always matter to a customer to some extent.

So in our Focused Office we are spending more time doing what our customers want, and we need to make sure that we are doing it properly. To make sure we are doing it properly, we monitor the quality, delivery and cost of what we do.

Important point number 2

In a Focused Office quality, delivery and cost always work together

Because the Focused Office cares so much about these three factors, it never improves one of them at the expense of either of the remaining two.

So just remember:

1 *Don't make staff redundant if that means quality or delivery will suffer;*

2 *Don't embark on a quality campaign if costs then go through the roof;*

3 *Don't take shortcuts just to get the job done on time, as quality will suffer.*

Measuring performance

In a Focused Office you know what the office is for. Because you monitor quality, delivery and cost, you know how well the office is doing.

With this in place, you can judge what everybody in the office does against the impact they have on the things that really matter.

Whoever your customer is, you can now tell whether what you do is useful by the effect it has on the quality, delivery and cost of the service performed for your customer.

If you want to change something, that change should have a purpose. And that purpose is always to improve quality, delivery or cost. As long as you always monitor the three important measures of performance, it is obvious if there is an improvement in at least one factor, without jeopardising the remaining two.

A quick review

Creating a Focused Office is the first step towards the Obvious Office.

In a Focused Office

- *It is obvious what the office does; it does something that a customer wants*

- *It is obvious how well the office is doing; you monitor quality, delivery and cost*

- *It is obvious who is doing useful work; do more of this*

- *It is obvious who is doing 'useless' work; do less of this*

Now that you have established a Focused Office, you can start making the office better at what it does. That means creating a Standardised Office.

Notes:

Notes:

The Obvious Office

Chapter Three

The Standardised Office

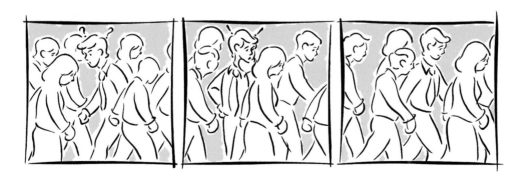

In the Standardised Office everybody goes about their work in the same way.

Why is this important?

Because if everybody does the work the same way:

- *the end result will be the same – the customer experiences consistent quality*
- *work is completed in the same amount of time – delivery is more regular*
- *you can work out more accurately how many people you need – planning is improved*
- *you establish an expectation of what should be achieved – performance can be monitored.*

In most offices the people who work there know very well what has to be done, but go about it in different ways. When everybody is doing the same job differently, you get different results.

Obviously, when people perform the same task differently they will not take the same time, and this will affect how much it costs to get the job done. But the main result of inconsistent methods is poor quality of outcome.

Poor quality

When people do tasks differently there are many ways in which the quality can suffer.

For example, if someone decides that it is quicker to type an address rather than using an address-finding utility, there is a greater risk of a typing error in the address. The person doing the typing may also tire more quickly, leading to further errors.

Differences can also happen at the keystroke level. Some people are confident using keyboard shortcuts while others have never learned, and still use a mouse to navigate.

Generally, keyboard shortcuts are quicker, more accurate and eliminate the movement of a hand to and from the mouse. Because the person using keyboard shortcuts expends less effort, more time is available to ensure good quality work.

Remember, speed isn't everything: someone may well be getting through the work more quickly, but at the expense of accuracy or legibility - which then causes problems for whoever receives the results of their work.

Dealing with customer concerns is an area fraught with problems, particularly where there is discretion around compensation. With complex systems, information relating to a particular problem can often be found in different places, which can result in completely different outcomes. Even if the facts can be established, unless decision guidelines are consistently followed, customers can still get different outcomes: they may be offered different levels of compensation, for example.

Creating a Standardised Office

There are two steps to creating a Standardised Office:

> 1 *Decide how you get things done*
>
> 2 *Make sure everybody in the office knows how to do things in this way.*

How to do something efficiently

Let's start by identifying the three basic steps that occur in any task.

To begin with, something happens that triggers the work: a letter arrives; someone rings in or sends an email; an electronic message or signal requires attention; a form hits your in-tray. It may be a date when an action regularly happens, or the minutes from a meeting. These triggers, together with any information they carry, are **INPUTS**.

At the end of the task, there is an **OUTCOME**: a payment; a completed report; a decision; an application approved; a claim denied.

The step you take to go from an **INPUT** to an **OUTCOME** is the **PROCESS**.

So when you decide on the best way to do a job, you define the **INPUT**, you define the **PROCESS** and you define the **OUTCOME**.

Where to start

Most offices perform a wide variety of tasks. These may be simple or complicated; frequent or rare; important or trivial.

Try to identify the tasks which occupy most people in the office, and those which have an important impact on the office's overall cost, quality or delivery. Put them into a priority order and work through them.

Try not to be tempted to rehash the procedure manual, though by all means use it as a check. Often the procedure manual is out of date and usually doesn't contain the all important job knowledge.

Please don't simply ask the office expert (for example, the person who 'knows everything' because they've worked there longest) to write down what they do. They may have gaps in their knowledge and understanding.

Teamwork works

You want to try and capture the best way of getting the job done, so use a team of people - a mix of experienced and new staff, ideally incorporating someone who knows nothing about the task.

Why this mix of people? Because you want to try and gather as many different points of view as possible, so that you can debate and choose the best method. The person on the team who knows nothing will ask the 'stupid' questions that often lead to a deeper insight into the process.

Give them time to sit down and agree step by step the current best way of doing the task.

Important point number 3

Use a group of people – experienced, inexperienced and ignorant – to decide the current best way of doing each task

Most people will agree in broad terms the major steps needed to complete the process, often involving between two and four major activities, for example:

get information → *review it* → *make a decision*
or
receive form → *enter onto computer* → *check for errors* → *file*

It is at the next level of detail that disagreements will occur, and these disagreements need to be resolved.

Ideally, a simple discussion and debate will resolve the conflict, but if there is any doubt about the best thing to do, then use data to inform the decision. Gather real data for the alternative methods and data about quality, cost and delivery, and then compare results. It should then be obvious which is the best method.

A common mistake is to go into too much detail when defining each step in the process. A complicated process with more than, say, 20 steps, with lots of decision points taking you down different paths, quickly becomes unwieldy and difficult to follow.

When this happens, reduce the number of steps by creating more general steps, summarising the detail found in the series of smaller steps. If it is worthwhile, you can describe the details of these summary steps in a separate document.

For very complicated processes you may finish with up to three levels of documentation: a high level showing major steps, a medium level showing more detail for some of the major steps, and a low level where fine detail is needed to adequately define how to get the job done. These documents are often presented as a flow chart or process map.

Document the process

You can use many standards to draw process maps, with specific shapes identifying such things as actions or decisions. Most important, though, is that the document is meaningful for people who use it - it doesn't have to conform to a particular standard.

Great! By now you should have an agreed sequence of actions that represent the current best way of getting the job done. Unfortunately nobody knows about it - which bring us to step two in the Standardised Office.

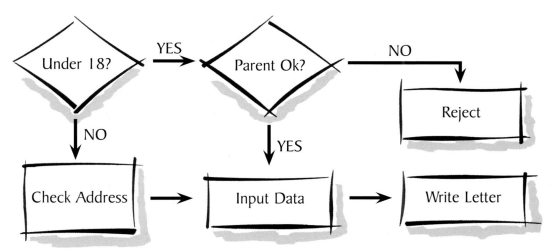

Communication, communication, communication

Having a defined current best way of doing something is, of course, completely useless unless it is put into practice. You must now communicate the new way of working to the people who will use it.

Choose the best method for making sure that people know and understand the new best way and can also use the process effectively. This may be:

- *as a formal training session*

- *at a team meeting*

- *during one-to-one coaching*

- *by simply handing out the information*

However you decide to disseminate the information, please make sure that the new current best way of working is thoroughly understood and that everybody is comfortable using it.

And whichever method you use to get the message across, you will always need materials that persuasively present the new way of working.

What do I mean by 'persuasively'? So that people can readily understand what to do, and can find and refer to the information whenever they're unsure about what to do next.

Sometimes the process map itself can be used, as long as it is properly edited so that it's simple to read and understand, and contains all the information needed to do the job properly.

More usually you will need a level of detail greater than in the process map to get the message across properly. This often means preparing a number of detailed guides to describe particular steps in the process. These guides are not procedures; procedures tell you what to do, but a guide will tell you how to do the job.

How to create a user guide

If the guides are going to be useful, they need to be **used**. And in order for the guides to be used, they must be readily accessible and easy to follow.

1 *Take great care in deciding on a format, whether it's a booklet, laminated cards, posters, the intranet, or whatever is most appropriate in your office. The most important thing is for people to easily be able to get hold of the guide that they need.*

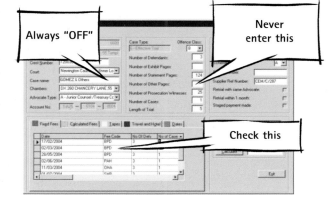

2 *Design matters. The use of colour, graphics, and different font styles and sizes can all help to bring the guide to life, and will make it easier to follow. Don't worry too much about the correct use of grammar - use bullet points rather than paragraphs, for example. You're trying to get information across as clearly as possible, not pass an English exam.*

An excellent test of a guide is to give it to somebody who has never done the task before, and see how they get on. If they perform the task well by following the guide then you know that it does what you want. If they struggle, it's time for a re-write.

A very simple example

An organisation I worked with wanted to establish a central pay unit for processing staff pay transactions. This is the process map developed for recording the start of a period of sickness.

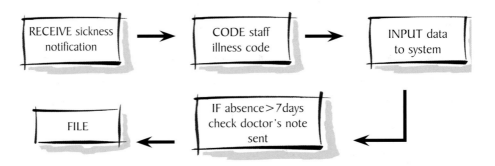

When we sat down to document the process, it quickly became obvious that people were handling cases involving the lack of a doctor's note in different ways. Some staff did not enter the sickness detail onto the computer until they had received the note, while others ignored the problem altogether because they had never been told what to do. The group agreed that in future they would update the computer before asking for a copy of the doctor's note.

Creating a central pay processing unit required new staff to be trained in each transaction. Staff were given a process map for each transaction together with a fully detailed user guide. And the outcome? Staff were not only trained more quickly in a standard process but actually reduced the error rates previously experienced.

The Obvious Office

Standard Operations

It's time to breathe a sigh of relief. Why? Because getting people in the office to perform tasks using the best current method is the single most important step towards creating an Obvious Office.

Once everybody is doing the work in the same way, the rate of work and the outcomes become more consistent, reducing variability in cost and quality.

If for whatever reason you have to deviate from the standard process, then this should now be obvious. You can find out why this happened and then take steps to stop it happening again. You have identified an opportunity to further improve performance.

Now that you have a standard operation you can:

- *establish reasonable expectations for performance (the quality of outcome and the time it takes) for individuals, teams and the office as a whole*

- *monitor performance over time*

- *predict more accurately how long work will take*

- *easily check that people are working correctly*

- *ensure that performance is repeatable and sustainable*

A quick review

Creating a Standardised Office is the second step towards the Obvious Office.

You already have a Focused Office where

1 *it is obvious what the office does; it does something that a customer wants*

2 *it is obvious how well the office is doing; you monitor quality, delivery and cost*

3 *it is obvious who is doing useful work*

4 *it is obvious who is doing 'useless' work*

Now that you have also established a Standardised Office, you can start to enjoy repeatable and sustainable performance, and should immediately see an improvement in quality, cost and delivery. In your Standardised and Focused Office, you are now confident that staff are working in a consistent way to deliver for their customers.

Repeatable and sustainable performance means that you can predict the people needed to get through the work with confidence. The next step is to create a Planned Office.

Notes:

Notes:

Chapter Four

The Planned Office

Do you ever arrive at work only to find yourself faced with a mountain of work that, with the best will in the world, you can't possibly get done on time? How do you deal with it? Maybe you try and find a quick 'solution' to the problem, such as:

- *seeing if you can borrow people from elsewhere*

- *leaning on staff to work through their breaks or stay late*

- *cutting a few corners to get the job done more quickly*

- *negotiating a later delivery for some of the work*

- *having a few meetings to decide how you are going to cope*

And then you find out that a couple of critical team members are on holiday.

Is this stressful or not? Does this encourage doing work properly, on time and at the right cost? I don't think so.

Alternatively - and I know this is rare - everybody's in and at their desks, and there isn't enough work to keep them going through the day. What do you do now?

You could ignore the problem and give everybody a quiet spell, but is this what they're paid for? How do the people next door feel watching your office playing desktop ping pong? And what will your boss think if he or she walks in?

Resource Plan

Whether you have too much work or not enough, the problem is created by not having the right level of resource to do the work on hand. You lack a realistic plan which ensures that the right people are at work at the right time.

A Planned Office deals with this problem by understanding more about the volumes of work arriving, and working out how many people are needed to get the work done on time.

The Planned Office has a **resource plan** that attempts to match the amount of work needed to be done to the people at work to get the work done. A resource plan tries to balance resource with demand.

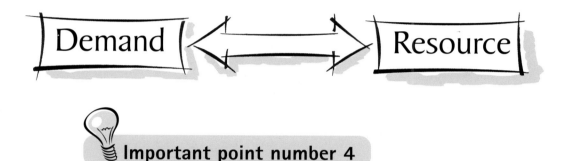

Important point number 4

Failing to plan means you are planning to fail

Remember the Standardised Office?

Whether you're working on the resource side or the demand side of the problem, the common piece of data needed is how long it takes to do the task.

Because you are now working in a Standardised Office, with everybody doing tasks the same way, this is easily established. In the absence of anything more detailed, divide the number of hours worked in the office by the number of tasks completed in that period. If you're lucky enough to have more accurate times - perhaps for each element of the task - use these.

Understanding Demand

Let's start with the demand put on the office. This is simply the number of tasks expected to be completed multiplied by the time it takes to do them.

Demand = Number of tasks X time to do one task

All you have to do now is predict the volume of work coming into the office over time, and you can quickly calculate how much time is needed to get the work done.

If only it was that simple! Very few offices have the luxury of work arriving in a steady and predictable stream; there are always peaks and troughs in workload. To do a better job of planning the office, you need to understand how the volume of work coming into the office changes over a period of time. With this information you can predict the number of tasks and then calculate demand.

Forecasting

The only thing you can guarantee about a forecast it that it will be wrong. Your job is to make the forecast as accurate as possible.

Where do you start?

Begin by looking at history. But remember that work completed by the office is not always the same as work arriving in the office. You may always have a peak of incoming work, but spread that work out over time

If you don't have history, start collecting information about how much work arrives in the office now: you can always refine a forecast as more data becomes available.

When looking at the amount of work coming into the office you are looking for trends.

Repeating trends

A trend may be cyclical. A common cycle in an office is a month, usually caused by organisations working on a monthly cycle of activity. So you will often find a quiet start to the month followed by a mad panic at the end of the month.

You can, however, find cyclical trends over a year or more, within a week and even within a day. Just ask people who work in call centres when the busy and quiet times of the day are.

Long and short-term trends

There may be a long-term trend leading to increasing or decreasing volumes of work. You may be able to use 'inside' knowledge to predict a long-term trend, which is often driven by economic activity or by the organisation itself. Sometimes, however, there is no immediately obvious cause for

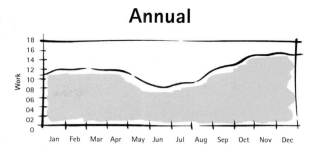

Annual

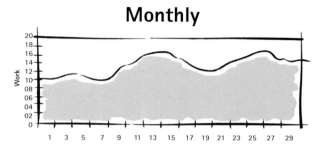

Monthly

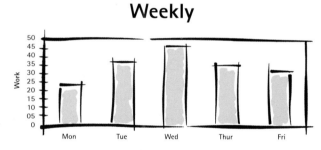

Weekly

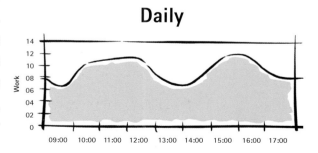

Daily

fluctuations in the volume of work over a period of time.

Although a forecast will inevitably be wrong to some extent, it is better to have an incorrect plan than no plan at all. As time goes on, the demand forecast should get better as more data is collected.

Calculating resource

In the vast majority of offices, 'resource' means people.

Some offices may have specialist equipment such as high-speed scanners or enveloping machines that might be a critical resource, and restrict work being completed on time. If that is the case then you will also need to calculate how much of this resource you have, as well as the people resource.

You now have a good idea of what work is expected in a certain period. So the next thing you need to know is how much work the office can do. For this you will need to collect some more data about your staff:

1 *Who works in the office?*

2 *What are their working hours?*

3 *What tasks can they perform properly?*

4 *When are they taking holiday?*

5 *Who is on sick leave?*

6 *What is the usual level of absenteeism?*

7 *When are they training others or attending training?*

8 *How much work typically gets done?*

The last point is one that is often overlooked, but is vital for good resource planning.

You mustn't forget that people are unlikely to work every minute of every day on useful tasks. You need to adjust the hours at work to compensate for all the time lost attending meetings, getting the coffees, dealing with interruptions, waiting for the system to become available, working on something other than customer tasks... and all the other things that stop people spending every minute of every day actually working on the tasks that are important to the customer.

For example

hours worked in the office	250 hours
tasks completed	200 tasks
normal time to complete each task (without interruption)	1 hour
Normal work rate	$\dfrac{200 \times 1}{250} = .8$

With all this information you can now calculate the amount of work you expect to complete.

Resource = Number of hours in office X normal work rate

As long as this exactly matches the expected work coming into the office then you don't have anything to worry about. You can confidently predict that the work will be done on time and staff will have enough time to do the job properly. Because of this, quality will be good; and because there is just enough work to keep people occupied, costs will be minimised.

Let's get real

Unfortunately, the real world isn't like that. It is extremely rare that the demand on an office exactly matches the resource day after day.

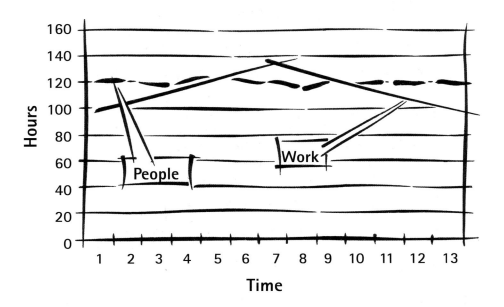

You will always need to do something to change either demand or resource so that they match as closely as possible.

You may be able to do something with demand by talking to your customer and arranging for work to arrive more steadily. It is much easier to plan resource if the demand is regular, but in many offices it is often impossible to change demand.

Usually when you try to match resource to demand, you will look at reorganising the resource to match demand. Why? Because you have more control over resource than you do demand.

Firstly, you need to decide, or influence, how many people should work in the office. Then you can:

1 *agree holidays so that more people are away during slack times, and as many people as possible are in when it's busy;*

2 *ask people to vary their working patterns or work overtime;*

3 *arrange temporary cover for someone who is going to be on sick leave for a while;*

4 *make life easier for yourself by making sure people are multi-skilled, so that when the one person that can do a particular task is away on their five-week holiday of a lifetime, their work doesn't pile up into an enormous mountain;*

5 *arrange meetings and training during expected quiet periods;*

6 *borrow people from other offices, or loan your excess out;*

7 *arrange for some temporary staff.*

When you try to match resource and demand, you usually have much more scope to vary the resource to match the demand than in trying to influence the amount of work coming into the office. So there you have it - the management mantra that people are an organisation's greatest asset really is true.

Flexibility

Getting work done properly and on time is so much easier when the people in the office can do a wide variety of tasks. This increases flexibility, helping you cope with unexpected absence or a sudden glut of one type of task.

It's a good idea to have a record of who can do what in the office, and also to keep track of how good they are at that task. When someone first learns a new job you do not expect them to do it as well as an experienced employee.

Eventually you do expect them to achieve the right level of output and quality. Check this objectively; do not rely on somebody's opinion. Once you know that someone can perform the task to the correct standard, you can confidently include them in the plan to get work done on time.

A real-life example

An office I worked with was responsible for performing a time-critical task. Work came in before staff arrived at the office and had to be completed and sent out on the day it arrived. Staff could not go home until the work for the day was complete.

The organisation was a good employer and its staff had many opportunities to vary their working hours. They could vary daily working hours, work specific days in the week and change their working hours to look after children.

When we analysed what work came in each day, we discovered a profile of work illustrated in the graph below:

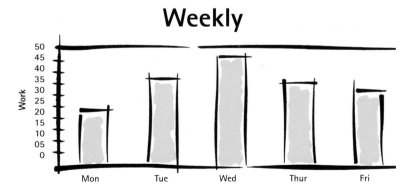

Obviously, Wednesday was a very busy day. More than twice the amount of work was done on Wednesdays compared with Mondays. Because the work had to be finished before anybody went home, there was an awful lot of overtime worked on Wednesdays.

Then we looked at how many hours were being worked on each day of the week. Guess which day staff avoided if they could? Yes, Wednesday. This meant that on the busiest day of the week, the fewest people came in to work. And when did we have most people in? That's right, Monday - when there was the least amount of work to do.

By explaining the situation to the team, we were very quickly able to rearrange people's working patterns to better match the workload. For the first time in years, staff went home on time on Wednesdays.

How the Planned Office works

In a planned office:

- **everybody** *is aware of the amount of work that is expected to be done*

- **everybody** *plays a part in making sure that the right number of people turn up for work*

- **everybody** *agrees to take holidays to minimise disruption*

- **everybody** *knows that unplanned short-term absence makes work harder for those who do turn up*

- **everybody** *has enough time to get the job done properly*

- **everybody** *has enough work to keep them busy, but not too busy*

A quick review

You now have:

1 **a Focused Office** *where everybody knows what they are at work to do;*

2 **a Standardised Office** *where everybody knows how to do each task;*

3 **a Planned Office** *where everybody has just enough time to do the work.*

You're confident that work will be done properly and on time, and you are monitoring quality, delivery and cost. Now you are ready to create an Organised Office.

 Important point number 5

Never forget the fundamental principle of Parkinson's Law "Work expands to fill available time"

Notes:

Notes:

Chapter Five

The Organised Office

How many times have you looked round the office and decided, "It's time to get this mess organised"? So you do a big tidy-up and put things away into desks and cabinets, label a few files and sort out the stationery cupboard.

It looks great for a day or so, but a few weeks later you might just as well not have bothered - the office looks exactly like it used to.

So what's different now?

By now you have a Standardised Office, where everybody does the same task in the same way, and so you can organise the office properly around the way work is done. Organising the office around the process makes doing the work easier. And if it makes someone's life easier they have a motive to keep it organised - and so the organised office stays organised.

But before you rush off to rearrange the desks and move the printers, make sure you know what you are trying to achieve by organising the office.

You work in the office to do something useful for your customers, and you do that work in a standard way. When you organise the office, you are trying to make it easier to do work.

The way the office is organised should be the same wherever the same task is worked. In the same way that you have sorted out one best current way of doing the work, there is one best way of organising the workspace.

The ⑤ Step Program

There are five stages to organising the office around the needs of the process:

① **S**ort out what you need to do
the work and get rid of the rest

② **S**et **in order** what you need to
do the work

③ **S**hine the workplace

④ **S**tandardise the organised office

⑤ **S**ustain the improvements made

These five stages are often known as '5S', and are actually derived from five Japanese words that begin with the letter S. The 5S program is used extensively in Japan and elsewhere to organise a workplace.

Always follow the five stages in the above order, otherwise you can easily waste a lot of time doing things unnecessarily.

① **S**ort

This is a ruthless review of everything you have in the office; if you need it to get the job done it stays, and everything else you get rid of. It's often easier to start on one part of the office and do it thoroughly, than attempt to get rid of stuff from everywhere in one fell swoop. But don't forget to cover the entire office eventually.

Look inside, on top of and behind all office furniture, including desk pedestals. What can you expect to find? How about:

- *obsolete files and unused manuals*

- *old forms, office memos and minutes of meetings*

- *magazines, often of a surprising nature*

- *long-lost staplers and bottles of correction fluid*

- *last week's leftover lunch*

- *enough pens to write War and Peace a hundred times*

Not to mention the 'hilarious' photographs of the office Christmas party, multiple boxes of paper clips, old envelopes...

Get rid of it

Anything you don't need to do the job you remove from the office. This is a critical review, so only keep what you absolutely need to do the job.

Just how many copies of that standard fax do you really need on hand? And how many pens can you write with at one time? Do you really need a selection box of pens of all colours and types?

Don't forget to review the need for furniture and equipment. If you only need one printer, why have one on every desk? And as you no longer use microfiche, how about ditching the microfiche reader gathering dust in the corner?

② Set in order

Once you have got rid of everything you don't need, 'set in order' becomes a lot easier - there is less to put away, so there is less to do.

This step can be summarised as 'a place for everything and everything in its place'

However, this means a lot more than just finding a home for everything. You must also decide the best place for everything in the office. Don't forget that the office is there to perform a process - and to make life easier, the office needs to be organised around the process.

A few things to bear in mind when deciding where things should go:-

1 *Think carefully about the position and relationship of the furniture*

2 *Reduce the amount of walking and movement of work from one place to another*

3 *Put sequential steps in the process close to each other*

4 *Keep frequently-used items close to hand*

5 *If space is a problem, keep rarely-used items away from the workstation*

6 *Make sure things that are used in sequence are stored in the right order*

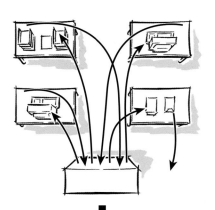

It's often helpful to imagine work flowing through the office. The office is then arranged so that the flow of work is not impeded.

There is one striking benefit from 'set in order'. If everything is in its place, you know at a glance that work can proceed.

It is also obvious if something is missing. If something is missing, then at some point work will inevitably be delayed.

becomes

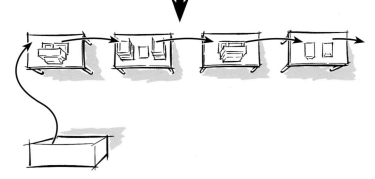

Now, problems like this are visible to everyone, often before they actually hamper work. The chances are someone will spot them, and do something about them.

③ Shine

Shine the workplace means cleaning the workplace.

This is much more than keeping things clean so that the office is a pleasant place to work. The act of cleaning will also highlight and reduce problems that might hinder the workflow. Think of cleaning as an inspection of the workplace.

Removing accumulations of dust reduces the risk of computer failure. (One speck of dust can stop a hard disk in its tracks and make the PC unusable.) A paperclip getting into a keyboard can disable one or more keys. Getting rid of finger marks and grime from a screen makes it easier to read.

As you clean around desks and cabinets you will spot more problems. Telephone, network or power cables can become trapped under furniture. Inevitably the cable will be damaged. Once the cable is damaged, at some point it will fail, leading to network, power or telephone failure.

Connectors and sockets are frequently damaged by furniture.

You might even find missing items of work!

Spotting problems gives you a chance to fix them before something actually stops working - and with a bit of luck, the task will be done with the minimum disruption to day-to-day work.

④ Standardise

Standardise means establishing the changes you have made as the norm. If there is a best current way of organising office furniture or a desk layout to get the job done well, you need to make sure that people stick with it.

Standardisation reinforces the best way to organise the office by documenting and communicating the way the office is organised.

The documentation can be:

- *photographs of different parts of the office*

- *diagrams of the new layout*

- *a list of do's and don'ts*

- *anything else that gets the message across*

Your goal is to make sure that it is crystal clear how a desk or a filing cabinet or a part of the office is organised to help people get the work done as easily as possible. Making the standard visible is a great help.

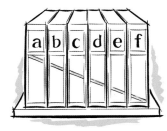

⑤ Sustain

Sustain is the final, and most important, stage of the 5S program.

It's pointless to clear rubbish out of the office if six months later work is again hindered by all the clutter that has accumulated. And performance will suffer if, having agreed the best way to organise the workplace to get work done, someone decides to organise things differently.

However, it could be that this person has a better way of organising their workspace. So there needs to be a mechanism to decide if it is an improvement, and make that the new standard.

The Sustain stage has two parts. Firstly, you'll probably need a regular audit of the important elements of the organised office. This audit will ask questions like:

- *is the agreed layout being used?*

- *are the files properly maintained and stored?*

- *are desks regularly cleaned?*

- *is the stock of paper by the printer being maintained at the right level?*

As long as this audit has a score, the results can become a measure of how well the office is organised. This then becomes a performance measure in its own right.

The second stage is to set a target for improvement. This will encourage people in the office to look for better ways of organising things. In this way, ideas that make things better become the new standard to be maintained.

And don't forget that you organised the office to do work better - so any improvement in the office organisation will mean even better performance.

Let's look at an example

Three people worked on the same task at a cluster of desks sharing a printer. Every computer transaction generated a print and after about 10 transactions, one of them would stand up, go to the printer, sort out their own work from the printer output tray and return to their desk.

Then

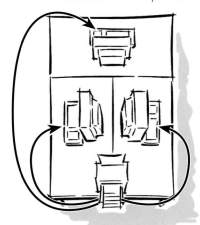

When the staff reviewed the layout, they recognised that time was spent walking to and from the printer and sorting through all the print-outs to find their own, so they came up with this revised layout.

Now

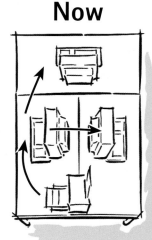

Simply by turning the printer through 90 degrees means that one person can now sort through the printer output without moving from their chair. As that person sorts through the print-outs, they hand on the work belonging to their two colleagues. And the end result? No more walking to the printer at all, and only one person rather than three people sorting through the work.

This simple measure - moving a printer - created an increase in throughput of more than five per cent.

A quick review

In an Organised Office:- `

- *you always know where things are;*

- *you only have what you need to do the job;*

- *stuff is kept in the best location to get the job done well;*

- *you can tell if something is missing or out of place;*

- *you can see where work is held up or running out.*

For most people used to working in typical offices, this sounds like paradise - and it is! But organising the office around key processes takes drive and commitment, together with the discipline to maintain the new status quo.

Over time, though, keeping the office properly organised becomes part of the culture. You'll find that 'a place for everything and everything in its place' has become second nature.

Notes:

Chapter Six

The Visual Office

People in offices are overwhelmed by information, yet they often don't know what's actually going on in the office, where things are, who is doing what task, or how the office is performing.

In the Visual Office important information is displayed so that it can be seen.

Why? Because whichever way you look at it, the human eye is pretty amazing. It can detect the light of a candle a mile away; distinguish between 17,000 colours, and process 1.5 million messages simultaneously. To do this mechanically would take 250,000 television transmitters and receivers! Simply put, when it comes to receiving and processing information, there's nothing to touch the eye for speed and versatility.

Seeing is believing

The Visual Office takes advantage of the fantastic information-processing capacity of the eye by making visible as much information as possible. When information is visible, people in the office absorb it much more quickly and easily, and also find it harder to ignore.

Visible information is always available. It is not locked away in a desk or on a hard disc, nor is it the preserve of the select few who attend a meeting or are on the circulation list. Making important information visual helps communicate all that is essential for someone to do their job and do it well.

Important point number 6

Visual information communicates ideas quickly, cheaply and effectively

This is nothing new

You have already started to make information visible. Remember what you did in the Standardised Office?

When you create a guide explaining how to do a task, pictures and diagrams are much more useful than words. And it's easy to do. First, take a screen shot or a photocopy of a form, and show what information is put where. Next, add some important hints or tips that stand out from the main body of the guide. Then put a copy on the wall or on a desk.

User guides are easy to absorb, can be referred to quickly, and are much more effective than the traditional procedure manual. Just think how long it takes to find the manual, and then to look up the bit you want - when all you really want is a quick reminder of what to do next.

Visual organisation

Virtually everything you did to create the Organised Office is visual.

Once you have decided how a desk is best organised, take a picture and put it up somewhere. How do you know if the desk is properly organised? How do you know if anything is missing? By comparing it to the picture of how it should look.

Remember: **a place for everything and everything is in its place.**

You've gone to a lot of trouble deciding where things go, so make sure everything is labelled telling you what goes where. Now there can be no doubt about what should be there.

Is the space empty? The label tells you what's missing.

It doesn't even have to be a label. For example: you've decided where the right place is for a pair of scissors, a stapler, a staple remover and some adhesive tape. Stick an outline of each object where it usually goes, and you then know exactly what should be kept there. If the outline is empty, you know immediately what has got lost.

You can also unleash your inner creativity. Use colour to distinguish different types of work, or the different stages of a task. Decide what colour represents a particular type of work and keep it in filing boxes or plastic trays in that colour. Now it's easy to find that work and also to see how much work is waiting to be done.

Visual problem solving

Problems come in many forms. Some are hidden; others are abstract. Visualising a problem helps make it real, and often points the way to a solution.

Let's say you have a problem with forms being filled in badly, and you want to figure out which part of the form is causing the greatest difficulty. Make a large copy of the form, and place a red sticker on it wherever a problem is found. This will quickly tell you which part of the form is giving you the greatest problem.

This is called a rash diagram.

Seeing information

The real power of the Visual Office, though, comes from visualising management or supervisory information.

Let's look at some examples.

(1) Holidays

Most offices have some sort of rules about booking holidays, which usually include:

- *how many people can take their holiday at one time;*
- *which periods are to be avoided;*
- *how many days you can take in any one holiday.*

Visual offices show these rules on a prominently displayed holiday planner.

No-one needs to ask their boss if they can have a holiday or not at a certain time, because the planner tells them. It shows the holiday rules, if they have holiday outstanding, whether holidays are already booked, and who has booked them.

Has someone already booked the time you want off? Well, you can go and talk to them to try and work out a compromise.

Why does the holiday planner work so well? Taking all that information that is usually kept in a supervisor's desk or computer and putting it on a wall communicates the whole process of managing holidays.

It makes the management of holidays completely transparent: the whole team knows that the rules are being followed, and if there are exceptions they know why.

(2) Skills and training

If information about who is skilled to do what exists at all, it is usually on a supervisor's PC or in their head. Guess what happens if the supervisor's absence coincides with an unexpected shortage of staff? Chaos.

A staff Skills Matrix display will show who can do what, and to what standard: 'just trained', 'competent', 'capable of training others' and so on. Now anyone can decide who is going to do what, or what may not get done.

(3) Quality, delivery and cost – a reminder

Never forget *why* you are at work: to do something with the right quality, cost and delivery for your customer.

Yet nine times out of ten, people in the office hardly know how much work there is, what the plan is to get through the work, and how well they are doing. If you're lucky you might get told at a meeting - but this all too easily forgotten.

Imagine how different it is when this vital performance information is on constant display, so that everyone always knows what is going on.

	Input	Telephone	Complaints	Filing	Audit
Sara	Trainer	Trained	Competent	Competent	To Train
Simon	Competent	To Train	Competent	Trained	To Train
Saita	Competent	Competent	Trained	Competent	Trained
Sacha	Trained	To Train	To Train	To Train	To Train
Steph	Competent	Trained	Trained	Trained	Competent
Syd	Competent	Trained	To Train	Trained	To Train

Legend: | To Train   L Trained   U Competent   ⊓ Trainer

In the Visual Office you will see information making it clear how good or bad quality, delivery and cost are. Typically, you will see information about:

- *what the office trying to achieve, represented as goals or targets;*

- *performance measures covering quality, delivery and cost;*

- *how you are doing compared with your goals or targets;*

- *problems or difficulties hindering the achievement of the goals or targets.*

(4) Graphs

A fantastic way of presenting what can be complex information in a way that is easy to grasp. There are many types of graph to choose from to suit your need, such as:

- *straight line graphs that show trends, ideal for time-related information ;*

- *column charts, useful for identifying proportions within data - for example helping to identify the largest type of error;*

- *web diagrams and scatter charts which display data in a clear and easy to understand manner.*

A graph in action

A team of people in a financial services organisation was responsible for performing time-critical transactions. They promised their customers to move funds within two hours of receiving a faxed request. Not in itself a great problem, except that they never really knew when the faxes would arrive, although they could pretty much guarantee a surge two hours before the end of the day.

The supervisor's problem was knowing if he was keeping up or falling behind. It was a disaster to get behind, as this usually meant it was impossible to cope with the end-of-day rush. Together we came up with the answer: a workflow board showing the number of faxes received every hour and the number completed. This was the result:

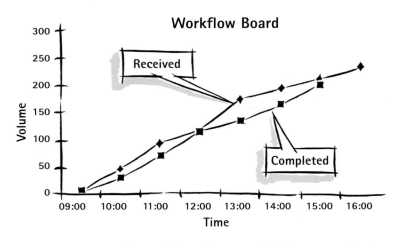

At a glance everybody in the team knew if they were keeping up or not. When there was only a small gap then staff could get on with other work. If the gap grew, simply asking additional staff to help out quickly improved things.

The workflow chart was initially a supervisor's tool, but since the information was public, the team quickly took ownership and started to manage their own workload and manning.

KISS again

When displaying this information you use the easiest and most visual method of getting the information across. Keep It Simple Stupid.

"well",   "not so good",   "where can I hide?"

The Obvious Office

How are we doing?

Simply colour-coding information red, amber or green can often tell you all you really need to know.

Cultural change

Creating a Visual Office is a significant step towards creating the Obvious Office. When you visualise how the office is organised, how it goes about its work, how well it is doing, and what the current problems are, everybody in the office is always aware of what is going on in the office.

And this changes the working culture. How?

- *presenting management information visually reduces the risk of confusion and doubt about what the office is for*

- *goals and measures are clear and unambiguous*

- *there is no argument about how well the office is performing*

- *information is seen by all to be open and unbiased*

- *finally this honesty encourages people to work towards the same purpose, helping to create a shared vision*

Visualising information is all about clear, concise, unambiguous and effective communication between people at work. Whether the communication is from supervisor downwards, from a worker upwards to their supervisor, or between groups of workers, communicating visually saves time, minimises the risk of confusion and misunderstanding, and fosters a cohesive and motivated working environment.

The Visual Office builds on the foundations of the Focused, Standardised and Organised Office to create a powerful, high-performance workplace.

Notes:

Notes:

Chapter Seven

The Improving Office

Congratulations ...

You have already made your office so much better!

Now you work in an office where:

1 *people do the same job in the same way – reducing the time taken and improving quality*

2 *resource is better planned - people have time to do the job properly*

3 *the office is organised around the process – it is easier to do the job*

4 *information is visualised – people can see what is important*

5 *there is no doubt what people are in the office to do*

And the result? Vastly improved

Quality

Delivery

Cost

You have probably found that motivation and job satisfaction are much higher as well. So... well done.

But there's more

An Obvious Office continues to improve, day after day, week after week, month after month, and year after year. It is also an Improving Office.

And what does improvement in the Obvious Office mean? It means constantly improving the quality, delivery and cost of the service the office provides.

The changes you have made so far have revolved around spending more time doing useful stuff, and organising the office so that it's easier to do the work.

In order to find further improvement opportunities, you now need to take a more structured approach. The key to this systematic improvement process is the concept of **waste** in the office.

Waste

Waste is anything you do that doesn't add value for the customer.

You spent a lot of time making sure that the Focused Office identifies who the real customer is and what you do for them. **Adding value** is everything you do that the customer wants you to do; everything else is waste.

Eliminating or reducing waste means that more time is available to do something for your customer, and will always result in an improved performance.

Important point number 7

Eliminating or reducing waste is the quickest, easiest, cheapest and most effective way of improving performance

As you have probably realised, you often can't see waste. It doesn't always end up in a bin. When time is wasted it simply disappears.

Fear not, waste always appears in one of the following forms:

1 Doing it wrong

Every time something is not done correctly first time, someone will have to put it right and the job is delayed – pure waste.

2 Motion

Walking to the printer or filing cabinet never adds value; arm movement at the desk may be necessary, but is still not actually adding value and is always waste.

3 Conveyance

Moving work from place to place is not progressing the job and therefore does not add value.

4 Waiting

Clearly, it's a complete waste of time if there are people with no work to do. But people can also wait for a printer to kick into life or a screen to refresh; and of course if the system is down or the network slow, more time is wasted.

5 Overprocessing

Whenever you do more than is absolutely necessary for the customer, you are wasting time and effort - more complete waste.

6 Building inventory

Wherever part-completed work sits in piles, whether physically or in a computer file, nothing is happening to it. And if nothing is happening to it, it might just as well not be there. Time that could be used more productively has been wasted getting the work to that stage.

7 Excess production

If you have delivered a service earlier than necessary, the customer is not inconvenienced. But time - and hence cost - has been used earlier than absolutely necessary. This is wasteful use of resources.

Identifying waste

If you look back on the changes you have already made in the office, in every case you have reduced or eliminated waste.

- **In the Focused Office** *you made sure everybody knew precisely what the office was there to do, and then identified everything else you did as waste*

- **In the Standardised Office** *you made sure everybody did work in the same way - the best current way - reducing both the risk of error and unnecessary actions*

- **In the Planned Office** *you matched resource to demand, reducing time spent waiting when there was insufficient work and reducing errors by giving people enough time to do the job properly*

- **In the Organised Office** *you arranged the office to minimise the time spent walking, moving and finding things*

- **In the Visual Office** *you made it easier for people to follow the principles already established, reducing the time spent waiting to find out how to do something. You also reduced time spent finding things and reduced errors by ensuring people knew how to do the job properly*

The Organised Office revisited

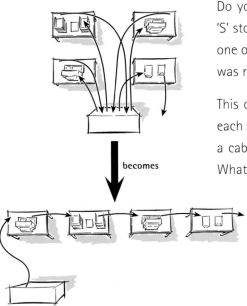

becomes

Do you remember the '5S' in Chapter 5? The second 'S' stood for **Set in order.** Let's have another look at one of the examples there and identify the waste that was reduced.

This office took 10 days to process a payment. After each stage the documents were carefully filed away in a cabinet, and then taken out later for further work. What types of waste are there here?

1 **Conveyance** - *the documents are carried to and from the cabinets*

2 **Inventory** - *there is a lot of work in the office, about 10 days' worth*

3 Motion - *people walk to and from the cabinets*

The staff redesigned the office layout in order to reduce or eliminate these three types of waste. Under the new design, as the document completes each stage it now passes straight on to the next stage until the process is complete.

What is the reduction in waste?

 1 Conveyance - *reduced from nearly 100m to 2 or 3m*

 2 Inventory - *reduced from about 10 days to less than one day*

 3 Motion - *virtually eliminated*

And the effect on quality, delivery and cost?

Well, stopping all that walking around means that staff can now spend more time processing the documents, doing useful work. Reducing the inventory means that work is now completed on the day of receipt, not 10 days later. And because people now work together, quality problems are noticed and resolved much more quickly.

This team are now doing more than twice the work they did before, reducing waste. They're doing it in one day rather than 10, and external quality problems have almost disappeared.

Waste is everywhere

Now that you know how to identify waste in the office, you will see it everywhere - and you will find it difficult to decide which type of waste to tackle first.

What you need is information that helps you decide what will give you the greatest benefit in return for the least effort.

You will need data about the amount of existing waste, and an idea of what needs to happen to reduce or eliminate it. Data helps you make the best decision. Why? Because it reduces the impact of personal opinions on decision making.

Important point number 8

Do it with data

When you decide how to spend time to reduce waste, you need to know three things:

1 *the likely impact of reducing the waste;*

2 *how long it will take;*

3 *how much it will cost.*

If you don't know, then make an estimate or decide to do a bit more work to find out.

If the benefit from reducing the waste does not justify the time and cost, look at reducing another type of waste instead.

Structured problem solving

When you set out to reduce or eliminate a particular example of waste, you are actually trying to solve a problem such as:

• **why** *do we make so many mistakes?*

• **why** *do we walk so far to collect prints?*

- **why** *do we have to work overtime?*

Organisations have a poor track record of fixing problems. They may do something that makes the problem go away, but all too often it just comes back again. To fix a problem for good, you have to identify and resolve the **root cause** of the problem.

There are several problem-solving methods you can use. They all follow the same basic logic:

1 *collect data about the problem;*

2 *find the root cause;*

3 *test solutions;*

4 *implement the best solution.*

No matter what problem-solving model you use, always follow a structured problem-solving process, otherwise you could find yourself spending a lot of time achieving nothing. And always use a team to solve problems, as a team will invariably produce more creative solutions than an individual.

The team needs to consist of a mix of people, just like the team you chose to put together user guides in the Standardised Office. Try to include representatives of people who experience the problem at first hand, as well as technical experts. And don't forget to have someone to ask the stupid questions that often stimulate a different way of looking at the problem.

Step 1: write the problem down

- *make it crystal clear what the problem really is*

- *do not ascribe blame*

- *do not suggest a cause*

- *describe what aspect of performance will change, and by how much, when the problem is fixed*

- *create a deadline for completion*

Step 2: analyse the problem

- *collect data about the problem*

- *identify possible causes of the problem*

- *collect data about the causes*

- *identify the root cause of the problem*

Step 3: identify the solution

- *identify as many potential solutions as possible*

- *test potential solutions*

- *using your data, decide on the best solution*

Step 4: implement the solution

- *use a pilot if appropriate*

- *communicate the change - and keep communicating it*

- *check that the problem is solved and that performance has improved*

- *amend work documentation*

- *share new practice wherever it may be useful*

The best solution to the problem is often the solution that improves quality, delivery and cost all at the same time. A proposed solution that improves one element of performance, but makes one of the other elements worse, is not the right solution.

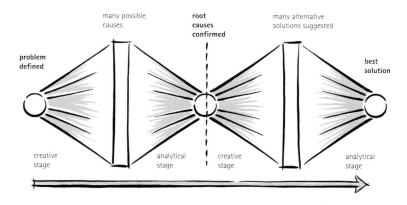

In the Improving Office, structured problem solving becomes a way of life; it becomes the way you normally do things in your office.

Why do you solve problems? To reduce waste.

Why do you want to reduce waste? To improve your performance, meaning quality, delivery and cost.

A blame-free culture

The more problems you identify, the more the office can improve. So you need to encourage staff to tell you what has gone wrong, or if anything is causing them difficulty.

If you want people to tell you when something has gone wrong or taken longer than normal, you may need to change the office culture. If someone comes to you with a problem and you respond with personal criticism, are they going to tell you about other problems? No.

You need to have a 'blame-free' culture. If personal performance causes a problem, deal with it later. For now, just solve the problem.

Believe it or not, you want to have lots of problems. The more problems you solve, the more quickly the office will improve. Train as many people as possible in problem-solving techniques and involve them in regular problem-solving sessions.

Structured problem solving can take many weeks, or it can be over in a few minutes. It all depends on the size of the problem. If you know that there will be spare time in the day, take the opportunity to ask a group of people to solve a problem that may be fixable in a short time. Big problems take longer, and you may need to use other tools to manage progress.

Remember, the more people who become adept at fixing problems, the more problems you can fix - and the faster the office will improve.

Measure all improvement in office performance in terms of **quality, delivery and cost.** The Improving Office monitors these obsessively to make sure that the benefits of removing waste through structured problem solving translate into real performance improvement.

Individual performance doesn't matter

It is crucial to realise that *office* performance is important, not individual performance.

Measuring the performance of individuals is relatively easy with computer-based work which can be measured automatically. But in some offices you will find staff slavishly recording what they have done and how long it took, so that a manager can assess how well the individual has performed.

Tackling poor performers has a minimal impact on overall office performance. Poor performers are counselled and helped, while the rest of the office makes sure that their numbers are good enough to keep the boss off their back. Systems that monitor individual performance often become a mechanism for justifying time spent at work.

And if you do succeed in improving someone's performance, that means just one person in the office will be doing better. Eliminating and reducing waste, on the other hand, will always improve the performance of everyone in the office.

By all means monitor an individual's performance if you have concerns, but don't collect data about everybody unless you actually use it to make the office perform better. Remember, people collecting and analysing data that doesn't help make the office measurably better is waste that needs to be reduced or eliminated.

A quick review

In the Improving Office, everybody who works there knows how well the office is satisfying its customers. They monitor quality, delivery and cost. People in the Improving Office also know how much better quality, delivery and cost are now, compared to the past.

More importantly, though, the Improving Office will have a list of problems to solve that will reduce or eliminate waste, leading to continuing improvement in performance into the future.

Notes:

Notes:

Chapter Eight

The Obvious Office

You now work in an Obvious Office. Imagine for a moment that you are a visitor to that office - someone who has little or no idea what the office is there to do. Maybe you're a member of staff from another part of the organisation. You could even be an outside technician called in to fix the vending machine. What do you see?

- *people*

- *desks*

- *cupboards*

- *cabinets*

- *notice boards*

- *a drinks machine*

- *printers*

- *at least one photocopier*

- *a computer on every desk*

...and there is still some paper around

So what's the difference?

Most people are at their desks, working.

If there is a group of people having a meeting, there will be a whiteboard or flipchart full of information to help the meeting, and the focus of that meeting will usually be, 'how can we do our work better?'

There may be somebody getting a round of drinks from the machine, but they will be on their own. An observer will rarely see people out of their seats going to get things like a file or a print-out, because the things they need to get the job done are close at hand.

Take a closer look

The office layout isn't regimented into lines or standard groups. Instead, the office furniture is laid out to make doing the work easier.

Desks may be arranged in lines, or back-to-back, or in circles or 'U'-shaped clusters. Maybe people aren't using desks at all, but are sitting at tables. It all depends on the type of work they're doing.

This office isn't laid out like a photograph from a furniture catalogue. Instead, it is laid out to:

- *minimise movement of people*

- *minimise movement of work*

- *encourage teamworking and flow of work*

The workplace is neat and tidy and only contains what is absolutely necessary to do the job. As most people can only write with one pen at a time, that means one pen per person. If more than one colour is necessary, one pen of each colour.

On a typical desk-top, there is:

- *a screen*

- *a keyboard*

- *a mouse and mouse mat*

- *the work in hand*

- *task-specific items, such as a user guide for that task, a calendar, a highlighter*

Inside the desk, you will find less frequently used items like:

- *envelopes*

- *blank forms*

- *telephone lists*

- *work-related personal documents such as appraisals, an employee handbook, a training record*

There are hardly any personal effects, unless they're kept in a bag that is taken home at the end of the day.

Where has all the paper gone?

In the Obvious Office, work rarely hangs around waiting for something to happen. Because the office is properly planned and organised, work is never held up by lack of resource.

Work doesn't sit there waiting for further information or for a correction or for somebody to do something elsewhere that allows the work to proceed. Why? Because in the Obvious Office problems are fixed, not ignored.

All sources of delay are documented, and the reasons for the delay are systematically resolved using problem-solving techniques, until all delays are eliminated. And because work in the office is completed quickly, there is less clutter and less filing.

Take a walk around

When you find work in the office, it will be clearly identified so that anyone can see what it is, and what stage it's at. It may be in a colour-coded file or tray, it may be in a bundle or a single sheet of paper, but there is never any doubt what it is and what happens to it next.

Because the work is well-organised and controlled, it is obvious if anything is out of place or mislaid. If one part of the process is experiencing a problem, work starts to pile up before that step. It is obvious something has gone wrong, either because there is nowhere to put work or because other people in the office slow down or stop because they can't move work on.

You will see what the office does. There may be signs over certain areas of the office telling you what goes on there. The user guides on the walls or on desks will have clear titles describing what people do. There is never any doubt what the office is for, and it's obvious to you - as it is to anyone visiting the office - precisely what happens and where.

Visual management

In the Obvious Office you will spot lots of stuff up on walls, whiteboards or notice boards, mainly about the work done in the office. You will see:

- *up-to-date holiday planners showing clearly who is away when, and what holiday slots are still available*

- *skills matrices describing who can do what in the office, and to what standard*

- *forecasts of future workloads*

- *problem logs recording issues that affect performance*

- *graphs showing current work, target completion and progress towards completion*

- *summary data showing current and past information on quality, delivery and cost*

- *celebration of success and frank recording of failure*

Information is presented in many different forms, in order to get the message across most effectively. How is office performance? The angry face or vivid red colour tells you straight away.

Loads of different graphs show how things are changing over time; some of them incorporate targets for future performance. Pictures of problems - like common input errors, examples of badly-completed forms, the damaged ream of paper or even the great spilt printer-cartridge disaster - replace a thousand words.

All this visual information is there to get the message across that the office is serious about doing the job well, and serious about doing the job better.

In the Obvious Office you can see whether the office is keeping up with work or not, you can see if it is meeting its quality, delivery and cost targets, and you can see that the office has improved.

How do you know that it will continue to improve? Because in the Obvious Office, no matter how good it is, there is always a list of problems, prominently displayed. These might include:

- *system downtime*

- *unforeseen absence*

- *poor quality of incoming work*

- *office-created errors*

- *excessive telephone queues*

- *printer failures*

- *poor quality photocopies*

Whatever the type of problem, it is always acknowledged and never hidden.

Alongside the list of problems you will always see a list of ideas raised by people who see opportunities to make an improvement. You will also see targets set for specific improvements where the problem and solution are currently unknown.

Once identified, all of these problems, ideas and targets become the core of the office improvement process. So in the Obvious Office you will also see a list of current and planned improvement activities tackling the most important issues in the office. Why? Because identifying and fixing problems will always improve performance.

The office will work on those problems that will give it the greatest improvement in performance in return for the least effort. This list of improvement activities includes a planned completion date and an estimate of the likely benefit.

Because so much information is prominently displayed, you can ask anybody in the office anything about their job or the office as a whole and they will tell you precisely what the office does how they do their job, what happens next and how well their team or the entire office is doing.

From dream to reality

Remember the dream I described in Chapter One?

"Wouldn't it be great if you could walk round your office and see how things are going? Suppose that instead of poring over computer reports and management accounts you could see at a glance if you were achieving delivery targets, maintaining service quality and keeping costs within budget.

"Wouldn't you love to know that performance will be maintained or even improved? Just think how much easier managing an office could be if problems were immediately apparent by just looking around the office..."

Now you know how to create an Obvious Office. You do it in stages by creating

1 a Focused Office

2 a Standardised Office

3 a Planned Office

4 an Organised Office

5 a Visual Office

6 an Improving Office

Will you have an easier life in an Obvious Office? No. You will work just as hard, if not harder, but the work you do will be highly effective and deliver real and obvious results - which will in turn motivate you and the other people in the office to go and do even more.

How long will it take? I can't tell you. It all depends on the size and type of your organisation and the willingness of people around you to take a radical look at what they do, and do something about it. But one thing is for sure: it will take forever unless you start **...RIGHT NOW**.

Notes:

Notes:

Don't Forget the Important Points

1 The purpose of the Focused Office is to do something for your customer

2 Quality, delivery and cost always work together

3 Use a group of people - experienced, inexperienced and ignorant - to decide the current best way of doing each task

4 Failing to plan means you are planning to fail

5 Visual information communicates ideas quickly cheaply and effectively

6 Eliminating or reducing waste is the quickest, easiest, cheapest and most effective way of improving performance

7 Do it with data

Resources

The use of the techniques described in The Obvious Office are very new in an office environment, and at the moment there are not many sources of help and information.

The Obvious Office website is being developed to provide information, help and support to people wanting to improve the way their office performs. It will collect case studies to provide more real examples of using the techniques described in this book. The site will also provide links to related websites, as more and more offices learn how powerful these techniques can be.

www.obviousoffice.com

Although The Obvious Office is deliberately written in jargon-free language, the six steps described are derived from tools and techniques used in two formal approaches to improving efficiency: Lean Management and Six Sigma. These techniques are now widely used in good manufacturing companies. If you want to understand more about these underlying principles, the following websites will be useful:

The iSixSigma website is a great source of information where you will find a wealth of articles that will help you understand what goes into a Six Sigma project. The DMAIC methodology is the Six Sigma formal problem-solving tool. Loads of information and links to keep you occupied for hours.

www.isixsigma.com

The Lean Enterprise Academy is a not-for-profit organisation established to develop knowledge of Lean thinking and practice, and to disseminate this knowledge through resources including publications and workshops. The website contains many useful articles and recommended publications. The Academy's founder and chairman, Dan Jones, has written some of the most important books about Lean.

www.leanuk.org

Notes:

Notes:

Notes:

The Obvious Office

Notes:

Notes:

The Obvious Office